First World War
and Army of Occupation
War Diary
France, Belgium and Germany

59 DIVISION
178 Infantry Brigade
Sherwood Foresters
(Nottinghamshire and Derbyshire Regiment)
2/8th Battalion
25 February 1917 - 30 January 1918

WO95/3025/8

The Naval & Military Press Ltd
www.nmarchive.com
Published in association with The National Archives

Published by

The Naval & Military Press Ltd

Unit 10 Ridgewood Industrial Park,

Uckfield, East Sussex,

TN22 5QE England

Tel: +44 (0) 1825 749494

www.naval-military-press.com

www.nmarchive.com

This diary has been reprinted in facsimile from the original. Any imperfections are inevitably reproduced and the quality may fall short of modern type and cartographic standards.

© **Crown Copyright**
Images reproduced by permission of The National Archives, London, England, 2015.

Contents

Document type	Place/Title	Date From	Date To
Heading	WO 3025 59th 178 1B 2-8th BN Notts & Derby Regt 1917 Feb-1918 Jan		
Heading	59th Division 178th Infy Bde 2-8th Bn Notts & Derby Regt Feb 1917-Jan 1918		
War Diary	Fovant.	25/02/1917	25/02/1917
War Diary	Southampton	26/02/1917	26/02/1917
War Diary	Havre	27/02/1917	27/02/1917
War Diary	Fovant.	27/02/1917	27/02/1917
War Diary	Folkestone	27/02/1917	27/02/1917
War Diary	Boulogne	27/02/1917	27/02/1917
War Diary	Saleux	28/02/1917	28/02/1917
War Diary	Havre Longueau	01/03/1917	28/03/1917
War Diary	Vraignes	29/03/1917	31/03/1917
War Diary	Vendelles	01/04/1917	03/04/1917
War Diary	Flechin	04/04/1917	10/04/1917
War Diary	Vraignes	11/04/1917	19/04/1917
War Diary	Grand Priel Woods (Fervigue Farm)	20/04/1917	22/04/1917
War Diary	Hervilly	23/04/1917	30/04/1917
Miscellaneous	Capture Of Strong Point R.26 April 1st-2nd 1917.	09/04/1917	09/04/1917
Operation(al) Order(s)	Operation Orders By Lieut-Colonel W. Coape Oates Commanding 2/8th Bn. Sherwood Foresters.	26/04/1917	26/04/1917
Miscellaneous	Report Of Operations Conducted By 2/8th Sherwood Foresters On 27-4-17 And 28-4-17.	29/04/1917	29/04/1917
War Diary	Hervilly.	01/05/1917	01/05/1917
War Diary	Hargicourt	02/05/1917	06/05/1917
War Diary	Hamelet	07/05/1917	19/05/1917
War Diary	Quarries In F.27.c	20/05/1917	31/05/1917
War Diary	Neuville.	01/06/1917	06/06/1917
War Diary	Havrincourt Wood.	08/06/1917	11/06/1917
War Diary	Equancourt	12/06/1917	22/06/1917
War Diary	Gouzeaucourt Wood.	22/06/1917	30/06/1917
Operation(al) Order(s)	Operations Orders No.11 Lieut-Colonel W. Coape Oates Commanding 2/8th Bn Sherwood Foresters	06/06/1917	06/06/1917
Miscellaneous	Operation Orders By Lieut-Colonel W. Coape Oates Commanding 2/8th Bn Sherwood Foresters	11/06/1917	11/06/1917
Operation(al) Order(s)	Operation Orders No 12 by Lieut-Colonel W. Coape Oates Commanding 2/8th Bn Sherwood Foresters	20/06/1917	20/06/1917
Operation(al) Order(s)	Operation Orders No.13. by Lieut-Colonel W. Coape Oates Commanding 2/8th Bn Sherwood Foresters	29/06/1917	29/06/1917
War Diary	Beaucamp	01/07/1917	08/07/1917
War Diary	Equancourt	09/07/1917	09/07/1917
War Diary	Le Mesnil	10/07/1917	24/08/1917
War Diary	Aveluy	25/08/1917	01/09/1917
War Diary	Wormhoudt	02/09/1917	20/09/1917
War Diary	Watou	20/09/1917	23/09/1917
War Diary	Brandhoek	24/09/1917	24/09/1917
War Diary	Wieltje	25/09/1917	30/09/1917
Miscellaneous	2/8th Battn. The Sherwood Foresters. War Diary, September 1917.		
War Diary	Vlamertinghe.	01/10/1917	01/10/1917

War Diary	Neufprt	02/10/1917	05/10/1917
War Diary	Dennebroeucq	06/10/1917	10/10/1917
War Diary	Sains-Les-Perns	11/10/1917	11/10/1917
War Diary	Perns	12/10/1917	12/10/1917
War Diary	Verdrell	13/10/1917	13/10/1917
War Diary	Petit Servins	14/10/1917	20/10/1917
War Diary	Alberta Camp.	21/10/1917	31/10/1917
War Diary	In The Field.	01/11/1917	30/11/1917
Miscellaneous	Appendix. Extract From X 59th Divisional Intelligence Summary, 2.11.1917		
War Diary	In The Field.	01/12/1917	31/12/1917
War Diary	Monts-En-Ternois.	01/01/1918	30/01/1918

WO 3025
59th 17&18
2-8th BN NOTTS + DERBY
Regt
1917 Feb – 1918 Jan

59TH DIVISION
178TH INFY BDE

2-8TH BN NOTTS & DERBY REGT

FEB 1917 - JAN 1918

DISBANDED

Army Form C. 2118.

WAR DIARY
or
INTELLIGENCE SUMMARY

(Erase heading not required.)

2/8th Bn. THE SHERWOOD FORESTERS.
FEBRUARY. 1917

Place	Date	Hour	Summary of Events and Information	Remarks and references to Appendices
FOVANT.	25th	8-30 a.m.	Transport left for HAVRE via SOUTHAMPTON under Major Martyn.	
SOUTHAMPTON	26th		Transport left SOUTHAMPTON on "Siptah"	
HAVRE	27th		Transport arrived HAVRE and marched to No. 2 Rest Camp.	
FOVANT.	27th	1 a.m	Headquarters & "D" Coy left FOVANT Railhead with 1 Coy of 2/7th S.F. on train.	
		2 a.m	"A", "B" & "C" Coys under Capt. H.P.G.Branston left FOVANT Railhead.	
FOLKESTONE		8-30 a.m.	Battalion arrived SHORNCLIFFE and marched to No. 3 Rest Camp, FOLKESTONE.	
		3p.m.	Embarked on "Arundel" for BOULOGNE.	
BOULOGNE		5-15 p.m.	Arrived BOULOGNE and marched to OSTOHOVE Rest Camp.	
SALEUX	28th	7 a.m.	Left Rest Camp for Station, entrained and proceeded to SALEUX	
		7 p.m.	Battalion billet in SALEUX and SALOUEL.	
HAVRE LONGUEAU	1st.		Transport left HAVRE for LONGUEAU by Rail where they marched to SALOUEL on the 1st.	

Hope Oate
Lieut- Colonel
Commanding
2/8 Sherwood Foresters

Army Form C. 2118.

Vol 2 of 3

WAR DIARY
or
INTELLIGENCE SUMMARY.
(Erase heading not required.)

Instructions regarding War Diaries and Intelligence Summaries are contained in F.S. Regs., Part II. and the Staff Manual respectively. Title pages will be prepared in manuscript.

2/8th Battn. THE SHERWOOD FORESTERS.
APRIL 1917.

Place	Date	Hour	Summary of Events and Information	Remarks and references to Appendices
	Mar: 28		Lieut: G.G.Elliot evacuated with German Measles.	
VRAIGNES	29		Battn: rested in morning. Moved off in afternoon to dig trenches behind post dug by 2/7th S.F. and 2/7th S.F. between FLECHIN & BERNES. Returned at 5=0 a.m.	
" "	30	3-30am	Commanding Officer rode out to inspect work. Huns shelled village in afternoon, direct hit on "A" Coy's Kitchen while cooking in progress. Shelled again in evening, "B" Coy 2 casualties (wounded)	
" "		9-30pm	"D" Coy paraded & marched to FLECHIN then moved in there. Shelled on the way up, two casualties SOYECOURT,	
" "	31		2/6th Bn. S.F. attacked VENDELLES from left, "D" Coy 2/8th S.F. from right. Our Artillery bombarded the village. "D" Coy in the village first, men coming through enemy Barrage well, 2 killed, 3 wounded. 2/6th Bn. S.F. went on to JEANCOURT but had to retire on 2/8th S.F. who had come up to VENDELLES in support. CONsolidated at VENDELLES, heavily shelled.	
VENDELLES	April 1		20 men & Lewis Gun sent to JEANCOURT with Lieut J.E.Broad to take up post in village. Lieut G.B.Logan took party to attack strong point at R.2.b. Captured position and took 1 prisoner, had to send for support, "C" & "B" Coys go up.	see Appendix "A"
" "	2		"A" & "C" Coys attack position at R.9.a. at 5 p.m. after short bombardment by heavies. "A" & "D" Coys dig in under fire of enemy artillery. Lieut. K.MacKinnon went out with small party Patrol and got sniper. Oxford & Bucks on our right & 177th Brigade on our left. 2/Lieut C.A.Cooper takes over post at JEANCOURT. 2/7th Bn. S.F. to make an attack on LE VERGUIR. Snipers busy all day. several casualties.	
" "	3		Commanding Officer & 2nd lieut: Drysdale went out at 3 a.m. to select positions for our snipers Enemy snipers got well in hand during day= 3 hits. Attack on LE VERGUIR by 2/7th S.F. fails. Major M.C.Martyn takes over Command of 2/7th Bn S.F. from Lt-Col: Rayner D.S.O. Relieved by 2/7th S.F. at 3-30 p.m. & marched to FLECHIN for rest. Lt:G.B.Logan wounded in knee & leg whilst out on patrol.	

A5834 Wt.W4973 M687 750,000 8/16 D.D.&L.Ltd. Forms/C.2118/13.

Army Form C. 2118.

WAR DIARY
or
INTELLIGENCE SUMMARY.
(Erase heading not required.)

(2)

Instructions regarding War Diaries and Intelligence Summaries are contained in F. S. Regs., Part II. and the Staff Manual respectively. Title pages will be prepared in manuscript.

Place	Date	Hour	Summary of Events and Information	Remarks and references to Appendices
FLECHIN	April 4		2/5th Bn. S.F. attacked LE VERGUIR, but failed to take it, badly cut up. Major Cursham suffering from Trench Feet, Capt. Dimock from exhaustion. Our casualties 3 killed 1 Officer & 18 O.R. wounded up to date.	
"	5		Brigadier-Genl. E.W.S.K.Maconchy leaves the Brigade. The Commanding Officer takes command of the Brigade until the arrival of the new Brigadier. 2/3th Bn. S.F. to attack LE VERGUIR to-morrow. Lieut K.MacKinnon & 2/Lieut M.B.Drysdale go out to reconnoitre	
"	6	9 p.m.	Plan of attack altered, 2/5th to attack ridge S.E. of LE VERGUIR in conjunction with 184th Infantry Brigade. Brigadier-General T.W.Stansfield D.S.O. new Brigadier. Lt-Col: W.Coape Oates in charge of Operations. Major M.C.Martyn M.C. in charge of Battalion. Battn marched off, in position at 11 p.m. Oxfords & Gloucesters on our right, 2/6th S.F. in support. "A" Coy (under XXLieut: E.C.F.Moffatt), & "B" Coy (under Captn. B.C.Huntsman) in first line. "D" Coy (under Capt. J.S.O.Oates) & "C" Coy (under 2/Lieut J.L.Warry) in second. Artillery started at 12 p.m., barrage supposed to lift at 12–40, but did a lot of damage amongst our men. Our men splendid.	
"	7		Got up to German wire but found it uncut, so commenced digging in. "B" Coy right on wire, therefore suffering most casualties. We lost 7 Officers & 110 Other Ranks killed, wounded, and missing. Oxs & Gloucesters withdrew at 4 a.m., our men ordered to withdraw and get back to FLECHIN. 2/5th S.F. very good in sending out Stretcher parties.	
"	8		Battn: resting & cleaning up. Stragglers coming in. "B" Coy go to VRAIGNES. "C" Coy at FLECHIN. Lieut: G.G.Elliot returned to duty & posted to "B" Coy. Captn. DIMOCK evacuated, unfit through exhaustion & exposure. Lieut: MOFFATT takes over "A" Coy 2/Lieut WARRY in charge of "C" Coy: MAJOR MARTYN M.C. returns to 2/7th Bn. S.F. GENERAL SANDBACH leaves Division.	
"	9		Enemy retired from LE VERGUIR & 2/5th Bn. S.F. enter. Party went out to collect our dead found 37 and brought them back for burial.	
"	10		H.Qs. & "D" Coy moved to VRAIGNES. "A" & "C" Coys remain at FLECHIN. Brigade relieved by 176th Brigade.	

Army Form C. 2118.

WAR DIARY
or
INTELLIGENCE SUMMARY

(Erase heading not required.) (3)

Instructions regarding War Diaries and Intelligence Summaries are contained in F. S. Regs., Part II. and the Staff Manual respectively. Title Pages will be prepared in manuscript.

Place	Date April	Hour	Summary of Events and Information	Remarks and references to Appendices
VRAIGNES	11		Inspection by the Brigadier-General. Commander "A" & "C" Coys come to VRAIGNES.	
"	12		Battalion on fatigues, and firing on range.	
"	13		Battalion under O's C.Coys:	
"	14		Inspection by the Divl. General.	
"	15		Church parade in morning.	
"	16		Battalion on fatigues. Officers & N.C.Os Scheme under Commander examined by the Brigadier-General.	
"	17		The Graves of Lieut: K.MacKinnon, 2/Lieuts Wilson & Viner located.	
"	18		The Commanding Officer, Adjutant & O's C.Coys go over to HESBECOURT to take over from the 4th Leicesters.	
"	19		Battn: moved to HESBECOURT. H.Qs in Chalk Pit E of HESBECOURT. "A" & "D" Coys in front line. "B" & "C" in support. 176th Brigade on our right.	
GRAND PRIEL WOODS (FERVIGUE FARM)	20		Companies digging Trenches, wiring & improving positions. 2/6th Bn. S.F. on our left & 2/7 & 2/5th Bns. S.F. in support.	
" "	21		H.Qs. moved to BROSSE WOODS. Enemy shelling our positions.	
" "	22		Relieved by 2/5th Bn. S.F. and moved back to HERVILLY. "C" Coy at HESBECOURT.	
HERVILLY	23		Men on fatigues. Officers go out reconnoitring near HARGICOURT. Plans of attack changed, 2/8th Bn. S.F. to attack Trenches in front of COLOGNE FARM and 2/6th Bn. S.F. the QUARRY. Party out on Patrol at HARGICOURT are gassed.	
" "	24		Brigadier-General's conference, attended by O's C.Coys: Practice assault at night.	
" "	25		Coys under O's C.Coys:	
"	26	11-55pm	Practice assault in morning. Cleaning up Billets. 2/Lieuts Page & Heath Join Battn: Battn moves off. See Appendix A	See Appx: B

Army Form C. 2118.

WAR DIARY
or
INTELLIGENCE SUMMARY

(Erase heading not required.)

Instructions regarding War Diaries and Intelligence Summaries are contained in F. S. Regs., Part II. and the Staff Manual respectively. Title Pages will be prepared in manuscript.

Place	Date	Hour	Summary of Events and Information	Remarks and references to Appendices
HERVILLY	April 28		Battn: Relieved by 2/7th Bn: S.F. and moved back to HERVILLY	
	29.		Men resting & cleaning up.	
	30		Inspection by the General Commanding the Division, and complimented on the work done. Battn: out on fatigue at night.	

K. Goodall. Lieut-Colonel.
Commanding
2/8th Bn. Sherwood Foresters.

COPY.

April 9th 1917.

To. The Adjutant.
From. O.C. "C" Coy.

Capture of Strong Point R.26
April 1st – 2nd 1917.

Sir/

I have the honour to inform you of the operations on R.26. Strong Point.

Lt. Logan in charge with 40 Riflemen – myself (2/Lt Warry) with 15 Bombers – advanced over the Railway cutting, up the right hand trench as far as trees marked on map. Here we met with strongly held position and heavy fire.

At the outset we killed two and wounded one (who was taken prisoner) and the enemy was seen leaving the trenches and running away from a commanding ridge on left. We held on with a view to consolidating, when w we found we were surrounded. With 15 men I fought my way back and established communication with rear. Meanwhile reinforcements had been sent for. Major Cursham arrived having passed through a very heavy barrage with "C" Coy, and simultaneously, Lt.Logan was compelled to withdraw from the two trees position.

Under Major Cursham's orders the Bombers advanced again to the position and met with slight opposition. Barricading was commenced, and Major Cursham decided that another Company was necessary to hold position. At his request "B" Coy under Capt. Woolley arrived as reinforcement. Meanwhile Major Cursham withdrew about 200 yards to avoid being cut off. The enemy then established a strong bombing post in the trench R.26.2.6. Major Cursham with Coy:Bombers and Sergt Walker attacked and drove enemy back. Sergt Walker proceeded 50 yards and barricaded with small party. M.Gs. were placed in commanding positions and at daybreak 2nd inst the position was strongly held by us.

I am pleased, Sir, to report no casualties whereas the enemy left 2 killed and 1 wounded taken prisoner.

I highly recommend the behaviour of Pte Taylor H. 3892 "D" Coy. Pte Overton 2922 "C" Coy, Battn. Bombers whose determination and coolness
(since wounded)
aided, in a marked way, the success of the operations.

I am, Sir, Your obedient servant.
(sd) J.Lucas Warry. 2/Lt.
O.C. "C" Coy.

OPERATION ORDERS
by
Lieut-Colonel W.Coape Oates
Commanding 2/8th Bn. Sherwood Foresters.

B

No. 5.

26th April 1917.

Ref. 62 C.N.E.

1. On morning of 27th April, the Battn will attack the QUARRIES and COLOGNE FARM in conjunction with 2/6th Bn. S.F.

2. The Battn: will attack on the left of the QUARRIES, its right on the road running from HARGICOURT to S of COLOGNE FARM.

3. Two objectives are allotted to this Battn:-
   1st objective :- First line German Trench where it meets road mentioned in para 2. at L.5.d.55.60 to where it cuts HARGICOURT road at L.5.d.95.45.
   2nd objective :- Second line German Trench from where it cuts road at L.6.c.25.45 to house at L.6.a.15.05.

4. DISPOSITION.
   "A" Coy will form 1st wave, and will go through to second objective.
   "C" Coy will form second wave, and will stay in first objective.
   "B" Coy will guard the flank, having one platoon in sunken Brick Field (Tennis Courts), at L.5.b.3.6. and other platoon in Switch Trench running N through L.5.b. and 29.d.
   "D" Coy will be in reserve in Sunken Road which runs N through L.5.b.

5. THE ATTACK.
   The front wave will consist of 4 platoons ("A" Coy) in two lines.
   The second wave will consist of 2 platoons ("C" Coy) in two lines.
   Bombers and Rifle Grenadiers will be on the flanks so that immediately the objectives are taken, bombers may establish Blocks to the left and if necessary, to the right, covered by the Rifle Grenadiers.
   "B" Coy will occupy their first position as soon as possible after arrival, and their second immediately after plus 16, at that time consolidating both posts.
   "D" Coy will be in reserve and will attack immediately if a German Counter attack is at all successful and if the O.C.Coy considers that there is a reasonable chance of success.
   "A" Coy will pass over first objective position and get ready to assault second position. On capturing second position they will push out Patrol and L.G. to left flank.

6. BARRAGE.
   The Barrage will play on first objective from Zero to plus 16 mins: when it will creep to second objective from which it will lift at plus 22 mins:

7. ROUTE TO POSITION OF DEPLOYMENT.
   HERVILLY - HESBECOURT (where "C" Coy will join the Battn:) Cross Roads L.15.a.7.9. Entrance to HARGICOURT L.4.c.9.3. from where 2/Lieut Drysdale and Snipers will lead the Coys through W half of HARGICOURT to L.5.b.3.5. then S to position of deployment. 2/Lieut Drysdale leading first platoon himself and detailing guides to other platoons.

8. BATTN: DUMP S.A.A. etc:- QUARRY. L.10.a.4.5.

9. BATTN: FORWARD DUMP :- Sunken Road in L.5.b.

10. FORWARD SIGNAL STATION :- Sunken Road in L.5.b.

11. BATTN: HEADQUARTERS :- Near Road at L.10.a.3.4.
    FIRST AID POST
12. ADVANCED BRIGADE HEADQUARTERS :- At L.7.d.77 RUELLES WOODS.

13. DRESS
    Fighting Order as suggested in S.S. 135 (Training of Divisions for Offensive Action) In addition each man will carry 1 pick or shovel and another sandbag. The Lewis Gunners will carry one pack each containing four magazines. (Haversack at side)
    The Rifle Grenadiers will carry 12 Rifle Grenades each.

P.T.O.

OPERATION ORDERS No. 5. (Cont'd).

14. POINTS.-
    (a) Mutual support.
    (b) Men close up behind the barrage may kneel only, not lie.
    (c) Grenades carried by the men will be formed into dumps in the trenches after the assault.
    (d) Consolidation.
    (e) Rifle and Lewis Gun fire for counter attack.
    (f) Waterbottles full to last 48 hours.
    (g) Men not to bunch.

15. Zero hour will be notified later (probably about 3-30)

16. Head of Battn: will pass exit HERVILLY at 4 hours before Zero. Order of March :- H.Qs. "A" "C" "B" "D" Coys. 50 paces between platoons.

17. There will be hot tea for the men at L.15.a.7.9. when Lewis Guns will be taken from the wagons.

18. Head of Battn: will pass W. entrance to HARGICOURT 1½ hours before Zero hour.

19. Quartermaster & Transport Officer will make arrangements for getting Field Kitchens, S.A.A.Wagons etc. to allotted places.

20. Packs will be stacked by Coys: and Quartermaster notified of place. Sick men will be left in charge, also to clean billets.

21. Two Signallers only per Company will take part in the attack.

22. 4 Battn: Runners to report to O.C. "D" Coy and accompany that Coy: Other Coys will send word to "D" Coy when they are in position of deployment, and Battn: runners will bring back word to Battn: H.Q.

23. Field Kitchens and L.G.Wagons will go with their Coys as far as L.15.a.7.9. Pack Ponies will go up as far as QUARRY from where their ammunition will be carried up by the Reserve Coy:

24. Coys will arrange for the Stretcher Bearers of each platoon to carry up the Rum Ration.

25. Rations and Water parties will come back to the QUARRY near Battn H.Qs. on the night 27/28th.

26. The Transport Officer will detail 1 limbered wagon to report at Battn: H.Qs. HERVILLY at 8 p.m. to-night 26th inst:

27. When the Lewis Guns have been taken out of the Wagons, Lieut Broad will bring on the wagons and dump the S.A.A. etc. at the Battn: Dump.

        (sd) A. E.Quibell.
               Captn. & Adjt.

Distribution:-
1-4 Retained
5. 178th Infantry Bde

(As per Routine Orders)

COPY.

B

REPORT of Operations conducted by 2/8th Sherwood Foresters
on 27-4-17 and 28-4-17.

Ref Sheet 62 C N.E.

DEPLOYMENT was smoothly conducted, and men were in position 2 mins before barrage commenced.

BARRAGE was splendidly accurate, and the margin of error on either side of the mark not more than 30^x.
It lifted at proper time, and the men openly expressed their appreciation of it.
No casualties were experienced prior to capture of first objective.
The Barrage drew away a little from the men between the two objectives, but that was not the fault of the artillery, but due to the fact that a wire fence, unmapped, stretched half way along the front of the assaulting 1st wave, which had to be hastily reformed after passing through. It stretched across the right half of the line of Advance.

WIRE CUT. Capt. C.P.Elliott, who commanded the 1st assaulting wave, states that the wire was very well cut in the first objective, but that there was only 1 gap in the 2nd objective, and that on the right. This Company had 58 casualties, largely because they could not get through the wire except on the right.

NARRATIVE. The 1st objective was easily reached and the enemy holding it bolted, on getting through the wire in front of the 2nd objective the leading wave came under a heavy enfilade fire from the right and left flank as at that time the 2/8 were in advance of the 2/6th, due to the fact that they had not so far to go, and consequently had both flanks more or less in the air. This Company had 58 casualties.
About 4-30 a.m. Capt. Elliott established touch with the 2/6 on his right.
As he found the 2nd objective untenable owing to their being no trench, and as he was losing men fast Capt. Elliott decided to withdraw to 1st objective and consolidate with "C" Coy who were already there.
Soon after this Captn Oates who was in command of the Reserve at the Sunken Road (3 Platoons) received a report from Capt. Elliott that the front line at 1st objective badly needed help. He sent one of his three platoons.
Immediately afterwards "B" Coy 1 platoon who had occupied the Switch Trench, were driven out by Counter Attack, Capt Oates at once sent Sergt.Walker and 1 platoon to retake it. This was done.
Capt Oates then proceeded across the open first to the Switch Trench and then to the front trench to satisfy himself that no further help was needed. This had to be done across the open, under heavy sniping fire, and it was done repeatedly during the day by this Officer.
Soon after 11 a.m. Capt Oates received a report from a Patrol that they had got into touch with 2/7th Post (vide Sketch).
Capt Oates now ordered Sgt Walker to go overland (there being no other way) from Switch Trench to Main Trench and bomb down towards "A" Coy, in front line, and to get touch, leaving a block on his left.
The Block was made but driven in. There were several casualties and Sgt Walker's party were cut off from the Switch.
Reinforcements were sent up and at 11 a.m. block was re-established. Next a block was established at Junction of Trenches from 1st and 2nd objectives (vide Sketch). Several of the enemy were killed here and 1 prisoner taken. Sgt Walker reported 2nd objective only spitlocked. During the operations a Patrol went out along 2nd objective to group of buildings N of COLOGNE Fm. They were fired at from Trench in front of building at F.6.a.00.
The Artillery were turned on to this, and next night the Patrol reported Trench obliterated.

2/

NARRATIVE.	On night of 27th Sgt Walker was sent to work down German Trench running E from junction of 1st & 2nd objectives towards MALAKOFF Fm. They were stopped by M.G. Sgt.Walker worked round it and blew it up with a Bomb. The carriage only is intact, the gun was destroyed, the former is being sent in and the 2/8th S.F. hope that they may receive it as a trophy after the war. Two or three men were killed here and Sgt Walker established a block 600^x W of unknown Fm. On the night of the 27th inst. a Patrol sent out by Capt. Elliott, who was now the only officer in the front line, ("A" & "C" Coys) reported that the enemy were occupying shell holes in front of 2nd objective, and a party was heard digging in behind. On 28th inst: patrol reported enemy digging in on ridge S of unknown Fm. Artillery were informed and registered during morning.
SHELLING.	There was heavy shelling at 8-30 p.m., 12 p.m. on 27th and 4930 a.m. on 28th.
REINFORCE-MENTS.	A Company of the 4th Lincolns came up in support on the night of 27th. They were kept in reserve at the Sunken Rd.
ENEMY CASUALTIES.	About 10 German dead were found, but a large quantity of blood etc was found at junction of Trenches from 1st & 2nd objectives, leading to the belief that a number of dead & wounded had been removed up this Trench.
OUR CASUALTIES.,	are 6 Officers - 3 of whom are killed (1 attached) and 111 N.C.Os and men. A number of dead not yet in - our band, who are stretcher bearers, are going for them to-night.

(signed) W.Coape Oates.
Lt-Colonel.
Commanding, 2/8th Sherwood Foresters.

April 29th 1917.
HERVILLY.

Army Form C. 2118.

WAR DIARY
or
INTELLIGENCE SUMMARY.
(Erase heading not required.)

Instructions regarding War Diaries and Intelligence Summaries are contained in F.S. Regs., Part II. and the Staff Manual respectively. Title pages will be prepared in manuscript.

2/8th Battn; THE SHERWOOD FORESTERS.
M A Y 1917.

K.3

Place	Date	Hour	Summary of Events and Information	Remarks and references to Appendices
HERMILLY.	1917 May. 1st		Morning:- Battalion practicing Rapid Wiring. Evening:- Take over Left Sub-Sector comprising HARGICOURT QUARRIES and Trenches in front of COLOGNE FARM from 2/7th S.F. "B", "C" & "D" Companies in front Line. "A" Coy: in Main Line of Resistance.	
HARGICOURT	2nd.		"C" Company attempt to establish Bombing Block at junction of Enfilade and New Trench, but find German Block there and strongly held, so make one at Sunken Road at L.5.b.9.6. "D" Company cut two gaps in wire in front of COLOGNE Farm.	
" "	3rd.		2/5th Bn: S.F. come up at 9 p.m. Two Companies occupy SWITCH Trench and L.5.b. to attack Trench in front of MALAKOFF Farm. Two Companies in HARGICOURT QUARRIES to attack COLOGNE Farmand Trench beyond. 2/5th capture both objectives on the left, but fail on the right. 2/8th Bn. S.F. establish Block at L.6.a.1.5. and touch with right of 2/6th Bn: S.F.	
" "	4th		Party of "A" Company walk into UNKNOWN Farm, L.6.a.0.0. by daylight. German deserter gives himself up.	
		8-15 pm	Germans put up a heavy barrage, and strong Counter Attack against UNKNOWN Farm, drive post out. 2/5th Bn: S.F. driven out of Trench in L.6.a. and F.30.c. 2/6th " " retire into SWITCH Trench. Colonel Oates makes arrangements for Counter Attack. 200 men from 2/7th Bn: S.F. placed at his disposal, but the Counter Attack is put off.	
" "	6th		Quiet. Relieved at night by 2/6th Bn: North Staffs: March back to HAMELET. Excellent Billets.	
HAMELET.	7th		Battn: resting: Capt: C.S.C.Oates goes to Brigade. Captn: J.E. Broad takes over "D" Coy: Lieut: H.O.F. Jeffcock comes from Brigade and takes over "C" Coy:	

Army Form C. 2118.

WAR DIARY
or
INTELLIGENCE SUMMARY.

(Erase heading not required.) (2)

Instructions regarding War Diaries and Intelligence
Summaries are contained in F. S. Regs., Part II.
and the Staff Manual respectively. Title pages
will be prepared in manuscript.

Place	Date	Hour	Summary of Events and Information	Remarks and references to Appendices
HAMELET.	1917 May. 8th.		Very wet: Inspections in Huts: The Divisional Commander goes round the lines in afternoon. 2/Lieuts. Profit and Wardle arrive as Reinforcements:	
"	9th		Battalion on Working Parties: 306892 L/Sgt Dilton & 307404 Pte Brightmore receive the Military Medal. Officers go to Lecture by Major Campbell on Bayonet Fighting at VRAIGNES:	
"	10th		First Trip to AMIENS, 3 Officers and 2 N.C.O's. Battalion Training.	
"	11th		Battalion on Working Parties.	
"	12th		Half the Battalion on Working Parties, the other half Training.	
"	13th	11-45am	Church Parade. The Brigadier gives cards of Recognition for Services rendered to 307264 Pte C. Buckland, 307199 Pte S.C.Billings, 305617 Sgt: F.Stanhope; and 306729 Pte C.Millon. 306293 L/Cpl G.Betteridge & 305960 Pte A.E.Johnson also awarded cards of Recognition but were in hospital at the time of presentation.	
"	14th		Battalion on Working Parties.	
"	15th		Men Training. Inspection by the Divisional Commander in afternoon, 307405 Corpl Hamer presented with the Military Medal.	
"	16th		Improvement of Billets. The Divisional General inspects the lines.	
"	17th		The Commanding Officer, Adjutant M's Weeds, ride out to the QUARRIES to see the new line.	
"	18th		The Commanding Officer, Adjutant & O's C.Coys go to the QUARRIES in F.27.c. and reconnoitre the BROWN line. The Divisional Commander and Brigadier kindly accept invitations. Regimental Sports.	
"	19th		Battalion moves to the QUARRIES in F.27.c. and comes direct under the Orders of the 5th Cavalry Division. Accommodation bad, men set to work well.	
QUARRIES in F.27.c.	20th		Companies allotted certain areas of the BROWN LINE to hold in case of attack, and to work on. Captain G.A. Duncan, Lancashire Fusiliers, reports as 2nd in Command.	

Army Form C. 2118.

WAR DIARY
or
INTELLIGENCE SUMMARY.   (3)

(Erase heading not required.)

Instructions regarding War Diaries and Intelligence Summaries are contained in F. S. Regs., Part II. and the Staff Manual respectively. Title pages will be prepared in manuscript.

Place	Date	Hour	Summary of Events and Information	Remarks and references to Appendices
QUARRIES in F.27.c.	1917 May 21st.		Battalion working on the BROWN Line. The Brigadier presents Ribands to Captn. E.C.Oates (D.S.O.) Private Gould (D.C.M.) Sergt Walker congratulated on being awarded Bar to D.C.M.; Sergt: Stockdale and Pte Delight also awarded the D.C.M. but unable to be presented owing to their being in Hospital.	
"	22nd		Battalion working on the BROWN LINE. 2/5th Bn. North Staffs: also comes to the QUARRIES. "B" Coy: move to LEMPIRE. Men wiring.	
"	24th		Battalion wiring the BROWN LINE. Orders to move to VILLERS FAUCON for four days wiring on the GREEN Line. Cancelled later.	
"	25th		"C" Coy: move to LEMPIRE. Men wiring on the BROWN LINE.	
"	26th		Men wiring on the BROWN Line. The Commanding Officer goes to C.Os' Conference at 4th Army School.	
"	27th		Battalion wiring BROWN LINE. Shell drops in "C" Coy's Mess at LEMPIRE, Lieut: Jeffcock and 2/Lieut: Curtis wounded, also C.S.M.Kitchen and two men.	
"	28th		QUARRIES Shelled in early morning. Captn: Moffatt badly wounded while getting the men out. Intelligence Officer goes to inspect the New Area. Battalion wiring on BROWN LINE.	
"	30th	5 am.	Transferred to 14th Corps. Battalion leaves the QUARRIES and goes to EQUANCOURT -1a TEMPLEUX and VILLERS FAUCON. Lieut: Jeffcock died of wounds.	
"	31st	9-50am	Battn: moves to NEUVILLE BOURJONVAL. Brigade in the Line, Battalion in reserve. Captn: Moffatt died of wounds. Men working at night on Communication Trench.	

M.W.Cull
Officer Commanding. Lieut-colonel.
2/8th Bn. THE SHERWOOD FORESTERS.

Army Form C. 2118.

WAR DIARY
or
INTELLIGENCE SUMMARY
(Erase heading not required.)

Instructions regarding War Diaries and Intelligence Summaries are contained in F.S. Regs., Part II. and the Staff Manual respectively. Title Pages will be prepared in manuscript.

Vol 5

2/8th Battn. THE SHERWOOD FORESTERS.
JUNE 1917.

Place	Date	Hour	Summary of Events and Information	Remarks and references to Appendices
NEUVILLE.	1.		Brigade in the Line. Battalion in Reserve. Working Parties.	
"	2.		Ditto.	
"	3.		Ditto. Reinforcing Draft of 56 arrive from 9th & 10th Sherwood Foresters.	
"	4.		Ditto.	
"	5.		Ditto.	
"	6.		The Battalion relieves the 2/7th S.F. on night 6/7th in the Left Sub-Sector of the Left Brigade Sector. "A" & "D" Coys: in the Front Line. Front Trenches which were occupied East of VILHAM FARM. "B" Coy: in Support. "C" Coy: in Reserve. 2/5th Bn. S.F. on our Right. 42nd Division on our Left. H.Qs. in HAVRINCOURT WOOD.	See App A
HAVRINCOURT WOOD.	8.		H.Qs. move to Q.10.d.2.8.	
	9. }		Ordinary routine Trench Warfare. Patrols sent out by Companies each night.	
	10. }			
	11.		Battalion relieved by 2/6th Bn. North Staffs. March back to EQUANCOURT.	See App B
EQUANCOURT	12.		Brigade in Reserve.	
	13 to 20.		Training, especially Lewis Gunners. Majority of "A" Coy. permanent Working Party at METZ. Draft of 56 under Special Instructors.	K.4
	20.		Brigade Sports.	
	21.		Brigade Rifle Meeting.	

Army Form C. 2118.

WAR DIARY
or
INTELLIGENCE SUMMARY. (2).
(Erase heading not required.)

Instructions regarding War Diaries and Intelligence Summaries are contained in F. S. Regs., Part II. and the Staff Manual respectively. Title pages will be prepared in manuscript.

Place	Date	Hour	Summary of Events and Information	Remarks and references to Appendices
EQUANCOURT	1917 June. 22.		The Battalion relieve the 2/4th Leicesters in Support in GOUZEAUCOURT WOOD.	See app "C"
GOUZEAUCOURT WOOD.	22 to 30		Battalion in Support in Right Brigade Sector in GOUZEAUCOURT WOOD. Working Parties in the Line. All men employed either by day or night.	See app "D"
	30.		The Battalion relieve the 2/7th Bn. S.F. on night 30th June/1st July in the Left Sub-Sector of the Right Brigade. "C" Coy & half "B" Coy in the Front line. Half "B" and 1 Platoon "D" Coy in the Support Line. 1 Platoon "D" Coy: in the 2nd Support Line. 1 Platoon "A" Coy: in the Reserve Line on the Right, and 1 Platoon "D" Coy in Reserve Line on the Left. 1 Platoon "A" Coy: in the Intermediate Line.	

M[?] Oate, Lieut-Colonel.
Commanding. 2/8th Bn. Sherwood Foresters.

OPERATION ORDERS   No. 11.
by
Lieut-Colonel W.Coape Oates.
Commanding 2/8th Bn. Sherwood Foresters.

6th June 1917.

Ref. Sheet 57.c.S.E.

1. The Battalion will relieve the 2/7th Bn. S.F. in the Left Sub-Sector to-night.
"D" Coy will be left Front.   "A" Coy. right front.
"B" Coy will be in Support.   "C" Coy. in Reserve.

2. ADVANCE PARTY. Battalion Sergt-Major. and 2 Runners. C.Ss.M. and 1 Runner per Coy: will parade at Battalion Headquarters at 4.30 p.m. and proceed to Headquarters, 2/7th Bn.S.F. and will take over stores.

3. The Battalion will parade at 8.30 p.m.
Order of March :- Headquarters. "D" "A" "B" & /C/ Coys. Headquarters will be clear of NEUVILLE BOURJONVAL at 8.30 p.m. Guides from the 2/7th S.F. will be at 2/7th Headquarters at 9.30 p.m.

4. "D" Coy. will take over Left Advance Posts.
"A" Coy. Right Advance Posts.

5. GARRISON OF POSTS. 1 L.G. & 4 men by day. 1 L.G. & 12 men by night. These Garrisons will be told off before the Battalion moves and march together.

6. FIELD KITCHENS. "C" Coy will take their Field Kitchen up with the Battalion. The other Field Kitchens will return to the Transport Lines under arrangements to be made by the Transport Officer.

7. RATIONS. To-morrow's Rations will be carried up with the Battn.

8. STORES. Officers' Valises, Picks & shovels, S.A.A. & all surplus stores will be placed in the garden near the Guard Tent by 6 p.m. to-day. The Transport Officer will make arrangements to have same removed to the Q.M.Stores.

9. All Shops and Sick men will be sent down to the Transport Lines. Nominal Rolls of Sick men so proceeding will be rendered by Coys: to reach Battn. Orderly Room by 4 p.m. this day.

10. TRANSPORT.
1 Field Kitchen (as per para 6) 1 Water Cart, 1 Limbered Wagon for Headquarters, 4 Coy: Lewis Gun Wagons, Mess Cart & M.O's Cart will proceed with the Battalion. The Transport Officer will detail the Wagons named to report at Battn. Headquarters by 7.30 p.m to-day. 4 Lewis Gun Limbers, Field Kitchen & M.O's Cart will remain with the Battalion.

                (sd)   A.H.Quibell.
                         Captn. & Adjt.

"B"

OPERATION ORDERS
by
Lieut-Colonel W.Coape Oates.
Commanding 2/8th Bn. Sherwood Foresters.   11.6.1917.

1. RELIEF.
"C" Coy: will be relieved this afternoon at 3.30 p.m. by "C" Coy of the 2/6th North Staffs.

2. GUIDES.
"C" Coy, Platoon & Coy. H.Q.guides will be at old Battn. H.Qs. at 3.15 p.m.   Guides for other Coys: will be at old Battn. H.Qs. at 9.15 p.m. (1 guide for each Platoon, 1 Guide for Coy H.Qs)

3. Companies will take over the Lines at EQUANCOURT from the Coys: that are relieving them.

4. Company Advance Parties will proceed with "C" Coy: and must ~~to~~ report to O.C. "C" Coy: by 3.15 p.m.   2/Lieut. Jones will accompany "C" Coy.   1 Watercart, 1 Lewis Gun Wagon and 1 Field Kitchen will proceed with this Company.

5. TRANSPORT.
3 Lewis Gun Limbers, 2 Limbers for H.Q. and Mess, Water cart (one) and horses for M.O's Cart.   Two limbers for H.Qs. & Mess are to be at present Battn. H.Qs. at 11 p.m.   The remainder of Transport is to be at old Battn. H.Qs. at 11 p.m.   Officers' Mess Stores must be at present Battn. H.Qs. by 11 p.m.

6. ORDER OF RELIEF.
The front line will be relieved first, then the Advance Posts.

7. The Q.M. and T.O. will arrange to move their lines in accordance with orders issued by Brigade.

8. The Q.M. will arrange with the T.O. that the Field Kitchens and Officers' Valises are moved to EQUANCOURT.
The Q.M. will take over the Camp at EQUANCOURT.

(sd)   A.H.Quibell.
         Captn. & Adjt.

"C"

OPERATION ORDERS No. 12.
by
Lieut-Colonel W.Coape Oates,
Commanding 2/8th Bn. Sherwood Foresters.

20 June 1917.

Ref. Sheet 57.c.S.E.

1. The Battalion will relieve the 2/4th Leicesters in Support in the Right Brigade Sector to-morrow, 21st inst.
   "D" Coy: relieves "B" in the front line.
   "A" & "B" Coys: relieve "C" & "D" Coys:
   "C" Coy: relieves "A" Coy:
   Relief will be carried out by 6 p.m.

2. ADVANCE PARTY.
   An Advance Party consisting of the R.S.M., 1 N.C.O. per Coy: 1 N.C.O. for Headquarters, The Signalling Officer and Signallers to take over the lines will parade at 9.0 a.m. and proceed to GOUZEAUCOURT WOOD. They will go via QUEENS CROSS.

3. The Battalion will move off at 2.30 p.m.
   Order of March as follows :- H.Qs. "C" "B" "A" & "D" Coys: 200 yards will be kept between platoons.
   O's.C.Coys will make arrangements for a good haversack ration to be carried for tea.

   O.C. "A" Coy will arrange for a guide to bring the remainder of his Coy: from METZ on their being relieved.
   Also a guide to take the Field Kitchens (see below) to QUEENS CROSS by 10 p.m.

4. TRANSPORT.
   The following Transport will go up after dark :-
   Field Kitchens, Wagon for H.Qs., Mess Cart, Medical Cart, 1 Water Cart and 2 Lewis Gun Wagons.
   A guide will meet them at QUEENS CROSS at 10 p.m.

   The Lewis Guns will be taken with the Battalion by Pack Ponies. Arrangements re Pans will be notified later.

5. STORES.
   Officers' Valises and mens' Sandbags will be returned to the Quartermaster's Stores. The Quartermaster will arrange for large sacks in which to put the Sandbags.

   He will also make arrangements for the removal of His Stores and all appurtenances.

   (sd) A.H.Quibell.
   Captn. & Adjt.

OPERATION ORDERS   No.15.
                                by
                    Lieut-Colonel W.Coape Oates,
                 Commanding 2/8th Bn. Sherwood Foresters.
                 ─────────────────────
                                                        29th June 1917.

1. The 2/8th Bn. S.F. will relieve the 2/7th Bn. S.F. in the Left
   Sub-sector of the Right Brigade on the night June 30th/July 1st.
   The line will be held as follows :-
   Front Line.   Half "B" Coy. on the right.   "C" Coy on the left.
   Support Line. (old Front Line) Half "B" Coy. 1 Platoon "D" Company.
   2nd Support Line. 1 Platoon "D" Coy. (This is on the left. There
                               is no 2nd support line on the Right)
   Reserve Line on the Right. 1 Platoon "A" Coy.
        ditto on the left.   1 Platoon "D" Coy.
   Intermediate Line.   1 Platoon "A" Coy.

   The platoon of "D" Company on the left in the first support line will
   be used to reinforce counter-attack on the Left. The Platoon of
   "D" Coy: in the 2nd Support Line will be Sergt. Walker's Platoon,
   and will be liable for use anywhere. Troops in the Reserve Line and
   Intermediate Line will not be used for counter-attacks unless
   orders are received from Battn. H.Qs.

2. Order of March :- H.Qs. "B" "C" "D" & "A" Coys:
   H.Qs. will be clear of the cross roads at Q.23.a 9.2. by 10.30 p.m.
   200 yards will be kept between Platoons. Guides from 2/7th S.F.
   will meet the Battalion where the road crosses the Intermediate
   Line at Q.17.b.9.5.

3. Lewis Gun Wagons.
   The L.G.Wagons will report at Coy: H.Qs. at 9.30 p.m. and will go
   up with Coys: They will not proceed further than BEAUCAMP from
   which point L.Gs. and L.G.Pans will be carried. 4 Guns and 24
   Buckets per Coy: will be taken up. The remainder at present with
   the Coys: will be sent to H.Qs. The L.G.Wagons returning from
   the line will take these back to Transport Lines.

4. Transport.
   1 Limbered Wagon, Officers' Mess Cart, 2 Watercarts and M.O's Cart
   will report at Battn. H.Qs. at 9.30 p.m.
   Field Kitchens will proceed to the Transport Lines anytime after
   9.30 p.m.

5. Water.
   All Petrol Tins will be carried on the L.G.Wagons. The Trabsport
   Officer will also make arrangements to send up all Petrol Tins
   from the Trabsport Lines. The converted Petrol Tins are to be
   divided amongst the Companies.

6. Two Dixies per Coy: will be sent up to BEAUCAMP and left at the
   R.E.Dump there in charge of the Military Police. The Sergt.Cook
   will detail 2 cooks to be in BEAUCAMP. The Q.M. will send up
   on Lewis Gun Limbers all Hot Food Containers, 1 per Coy: and 2 on
   H.Qs.Wagon. Some Hot Food Containers will be handed over by
   The Q.M. of the 2/7th to the Q.M. of this Unit at the Transport Lines

7. Rations.
   Rations for the next day will be carried on the men. The Q.M.
   will send them up as far as possible by day, carrying parties will
   take them up to Coys: the remainder of the way. Rations to be
   at Q.27.b.2.2. at 12.30 p.m.

8. SICK.
   Sick as detailed by the M.O. will proceed to the Transport Lines.

9. ADVANCE PARTY.
   The R.SM. and 1 N.C.O. per Coy: will leave Battn. H.QS. at 4 p.m.
   to take over stores.

10. Completion of Relief.
    When Relief has been completed Coys: will report to Battn. H.Qs.
    by the code word "BEER".

                        (sd)   A.H.Quibell.
                                    Captn. & Adjt.

Army Form C. 2118.

WAR DIARY
~~INTELLIGENCE SUMMARY~~
(Erase heading not required.)

Instructions regarding War Diaries and Intelligence Summaries are contained in F.S. Regs., Part II. and the Staff Manual respectively. Title Pages will be prepared in manuscript.

J.B.C.

R.5

Place	Date	Hour	Summary of Events and Information	Remarks and references to Appendices
	1917 July.		2/8th Battn. THE SHERWOOD FORESTERS. **JULY 1917.**	
BEAUCAMP	1.		Battalion in the Left Sub-Sector of the Right Brigade. "B" & "C" Coys in the Front line. "A" & "D" Coys in the Reserve Line. (1 Platoon of "D" Coy in support).	
	2 3		Ordinary Routine Trench Warfare	
	4.		"A" & "D" Coys relieve "B" & "C" Coys in Front Line. The platoon of "D" Coy remaining in support)	
	5. 6. 7. 8.		Ordinary Routine Trench Warfare. Fighting or Reconnoitring Patrols sent out by Coys each night. On the night of 8/9th the Battalion relieved by the 2/6th Bn.London Regt. (Half Battalion) and marched back to EQUANCOURT where it rested for the night.	
EQUANCOURT	9.		Battalion march from EQUANCOURT to Camp at LE MESNIL (O.35.d.central), where the Brigade concentrated. Divisional Headquarters at BARASTRE.	
LE MESNIL	10.		Battalion re-organised. Two platoons per Company being formed.	
	11 12 13 14.		Training. (Musketry and Lewis Gun Firing).	
	15.		Church Parades. Officers go over SOMME Battlefields from BAZENTIN to the BUTT DE WARLENCOURT.	
	16 to 20		Training. Brigade Tactical Exercise No. 1. carried out.	

Army Form C. 2118.

WAR DIARY
or
INTELLIGENCE SUMMARY
(Erase heading not required.) (2).

Place	Date	Hour	Summary of Events and Information	Remarks and references to Appendices
LE MESNIL	1917 July 21.		Divisional Sports at BARASTRE.	
	22		Church Parades.	
	23		Brigade engaged in Tactical Exercise.	
	25		Brigade Rifle Meeting at BARASTRE.	
	26		Training.	
	27		Divisional Tactical Exercise carried out.	
	28		Reinforcing Draft of 75 Other Ranks arrived. Brigade Race Meeting.	
	29		Church Parades.	
	30		Training. Draft of 75 under special instructors.	
	31		Battalion Scheme.	

H.Hapedale, Lieut-Colonel.
Commanding.
2/8th Bn. Sherwood Foresters.

Army Form C. 2118.

WAR DIARY
or
INTELLIGENCE SUMMARY

(Erase heading not required.)

2/8th Battn. THE SHERWOOD FORESTERS.
AUGUST 1917.

Place	Date	Hour	Summary of Events and Information	Remarks and references to Appendices
LE MESNIL.	1917 Augt 1 to 11.		Battalion Training, including night March, followed by Brigade Tactical Exercise on the morning of the 11th inst.	
	11		177th Brigade Race Meeting.	
	14 18		Reinforcing Draft of 38 Other Ranks arrived. ditto 120 ditto.	
	14 to 23		Battalion Training.	
	21 24		Reinforcing Draft of 50 Other Ranks. Battalion moved by Route March and Motor Bus to AVELUY.	
AVELUY.	25 to 30		Battalion Special Training.	

Hoskens Lieut-Colonel.
Commanding
2/8th Bn. Sherwood Foresters.

Army Form C. 2118.

WAR DIARY
or
INTELLIGENCE SUMMARY

(Erase heading not required.)

Vol 8

K.7

2/8th Battn. THE SHERWOOD FORESTERS.

SEPTEMBER 1917.

Place	Date	Hour	Summary of Events and Information	Remarks and references to Appendices
AVELUY	1917 Aug 31 1st Octr.	6.30pm	The Battalion entrain at BEAUCOURT and detrain at GODEWAERSVELDE at 4.30 p.m. 1st Octr. March via STEENVOORDE and WINNEZEELE to camp near WORMHOUDT, arriving 10 p.m.	
WORMHOUDT	2nd to 20th		Battalion and Brigade Training. Practicing new formations for Attack. (System of small Columns.	
	20th		Battalion march via STEENVOORDE and ABEELE to WATOU No.2 Area.	
WATOU	23rd		Move to BRANDHOEK No.2 Area.	
BRANDHOEK	24th		Battalion march to Forward Area, billeted in the Old British Front Line Trenches.	
WIELTJE	25th to 29th	11.30p.m.	The Battalion form up and move to the position of Assembly for the Attack	See Appx "A"
	30th		March back to camp at VLAMERTINGHE Battn. resting	

[signature]
Capt & Adjt
Major.
Officer Commanding.
2/8th Bn. Sherwood Foresters.

2/8th Battn. THE SHERWOOD FORESTERS.
WAR DIARY, SEPTEMBER 1917.
APPENDIX "A".

The Battalion moved off from the Old British Front Line about 11 p.m., 25th inst, to the Position of Assembly, just behind the Position of Assembly of the 2/7th Bn. Sherwood Foresters, i.e., West of SCHULER GALLERIES.

ZERO was 5.50 a.m. 26th inst, when the whole attack moved forward. The 2/7th Bn. Sherwood Foresters were detailed to take the ground as far East as FOKKER FARM. The 2/8th Bn. were then to pass through and take the ground as far East as RIVERSIDE. The Battalion Area was divided into three portions.

The Battalion formed up, "C" Coy in front, then "D" Coy, "A" Coy and then "B" Coy.

"C" Coy. were detailed to go through and capture the second portion of the ground, their line being as far East as TORONTO. "D" Coy were to go through and capture the remainder of the ground. "A" Coy to follow the attack closely to give assistance where necessary. "B" Coy, consisting of one platoon, to remain west of the road running North and South just West of TORONTO and act as Local Reserve. The other two platoons acted as Carrying Parties.

The attack went entirely according to Programme, all objectives were taken to time.

About 7 o'clock in the evening a German Counter-attack developed, which forced a little back the Division on the left, also the Battalion on the right, on our front it was broken by the Artillery fire, and our men did not give at all.

Very heavy Officer casualties were suffered, and it was necessary to bring Captn. C.P.Elliott and 2/Lieut G.R.MacDonald from the Transport Lines. Captn C.P.Elliott took over command of the Front Line early morning of the 27th inst, he himself was twice buried and had to be relieved on the morning of the 28th, when the position of the Battalion was Lieut G.G.Elliot, Signalling Officer, and 120 men holding the Front Line just short of RIVERSIDE, the Adjutant (Captn A.H.Quibell, D.S.O.) in command of forward Headquarters at TORONTO FARM, 2/Lieut. G.R.MacDonald with the Reserve Line 100 yards in rear, and the Regtl-Sgt-Major (W.H.King D.C.M.) acting as Adjutant with the Commanding Officer at Battalion Headquarters at CORN HILL. That night at 11 p.m. the 2/6th Bn. North Staffs took over and the Battalion was withdrawn into Reserve in CALL TRENCHES near WEILTJE.

On the return journey the Boche dropped a number of Gas Shells and the men had to march back with Gas Helmets on. The Boche stopped about 12 o'clock and the men got down to rest. About 4 a.m. the Boche gas-shelled CALL TRENCHES and owing to the exhaustion of the men and the difficulty in waking them the Battalion had about 100 slight cases of gas.

At 11 a.m. the Battalion marched back to No: 2 Area VLAMERTINGHE.

In the attack on the Right the 2/5th and 2/6th Battns Sherwood Foresters attacked, the 2/5th going through the 2/6th to the furth furthest objective, on the left the 2/12th London Regt. and of the 175th Brigade, 58th Division did the attack.

Our casualties were, Killed :- 2/Lieut J.G.Roe & 2/Lieut. H.A. HADDON, and 43 Other Ranks.

Wounded :- Capt. J.E.Broad, Captn. D.de B.Lipscomb, Capt. L.S.Bampton, Lieut W.H.Hayhoe, 2/Lieut F.Lewis, 2/Lieut A.L.Cook, 2/Lieut W.S.Jones, 2/Lieut L.Mellows, 2/Lieut E.N.Smith, 2/Lieut W.Charlesworth, 2/Lieut J.H.Hough. and 239 Other Ranks.

Died of Wounds :- 7 other Ranks. Missing :- 39 Other Ranks.

Gassed :- Lieut & Q.M. G.J.D.Schumach, The Revd. G.A.W. WILKINSON C.F. (attached) and 89 Other Ranks.

Army Form C. 2118.

WAR DIARY
or
INTELLIGENCE SUMMARY.
(Erase heading not required.)

2/8th Battn Sherwood Foresters.

OCTOBER 1917.

Place	Date	Hour	Summary of Events and Information	Remarks and references to Appendices
VLAMERTINGHE	1917 Oct 1st.	8.5 am	Battalion move by train to STEINBECQUE. (Battalion on the 1st train, Gators on the 2nd, and Waltrants on the 3rd) Transport move by Road.	
NEUFPRÉ	2 to 4		March from STEINBECQUE to billets at NEUFPRÉ and PECQUE. Battalion arrive 4 pm. Transport 6 am, 2nd inst. Battalion resting and reorganising.	
DENNEBROE-UEQ	5.		Battalion move to DENNEBROCUEQ, marching the first half of the journey and bus the second.	
	6, 7, 8, 9		Training.	
SAINS-LES-PERNS	10		Move to SAINS-LES-PERNS. } Division taking over from the Canadians in front of LENS and to the South.	
PERNS	11		Move to PERNS.	
VERDRELL	12		Move to VERDRELL.	
PETIT SERVINS	13.		Move to PETIT SERVINS.	
	14, 15, 16		Brigade in Reserve. Training. Working parties forward.	

Army Form C. 2118.

WAR DIARY /2
~~INTELLIGENCE SUMMARY.~~
(Erase heading not required.)

Instructions regarding War Diaries and Intelligence Summaries are contained in F. S. Regs., Part II. and the Staff Manual respectively. Title pages will be prepared in manuscript.

Place	Date 1917	Hour	Summary of Events and Information	Remarks and references to Appendices
PETIT SERVINS	Oct. 17 to 20.		Battalion move to ALBERTA Camp. SOUCHEZ. Working parties. Few men kept off for Special Classes in Bombing and Lewis Gun Work.	
ALBERTA Camp.	21/22		On night 21/22nd Battalion relieve 2/5" Leicesters (Battalion in Reserve) in Reserve to the right Brigade Sector of the Divisional Front. Ref sheet 36C S.W. Battalion H.Q.s in Piano Dugouts PRESCOTT ROAD (S.6.central). One Company at Batt'n H.Q.s. One Company in ANXIOUS TRENCH. One Company in RED TRENCH, and one Company at LA COULOTTE. 2/5" Batt'n = Right Front Batt'n. 2/6" " = Left " " 2/7" " = in Support. Working Parties on C.Ts.	
	29.		On night 29/30" Battalion move up and relieve 2/6" S.F. in left Sector of the Brigade frontage. 2/4" Roy S.F. on our Right. 179" Brigade on our left. "B" and "D" Coys under Capt. C.P. Elliott in the right Battalion Sector "C" and "A" Coys under Major F.G. Cunningham in the left Battalion Sector. Batt'n: H.Q.s at LA COULOTTE.	

Army Form C. 2118.

WAR DIARY/3.
or
INTELLIGENCE SUMMARY.
(Erase heading not required.)

Instructions regarding War Diaries and Intelligence Summaries are contained in F. S. Regs., Part II. and the Staff Manual respectively. Title pages will be prepared in manuscript.

Place	Date	Hour	Summary of Events and Information	Remarks and references to Appendices
	1917 Oct 29/31		Battalion front from N.33.a.0.3. to N.25.d.9.9. Boche make a raid on post at N.27.c.2.2.	See appdx

EM Duncan. Major.
Commanding
2/8' Bn Sherwood Foresters

Army Form C. 2118.

WAR DIARY
INTELLIGENCE SUMMARY.
(Erase heading not required.)

Instructions regarding War Diaries and Intelligence Summaries are contained in F.S. Regs., Part II. and the Staff Manual respectively. Title pages will be prepared in manuscript.

2/8 Notts Derby

Place	Date	Hour	Summary of Events and Information	Remarks and references to Appendices
In the Field.	1917 Novr. 1st to 5th		Battalion holding the Line in Avion Sector.	
	6th		Relieved by the 2/5th Bn. North Staffs. Battn. brought down from RED Trench on Light Railway to CHATEAU de la HAIE, and marched to GOUY SERVINS.	
	7th to 13th		Battalion resting at GOUY SERVINS. Training carried out, including Tactical Schemes.	
	13th		Ceremonial Parade at CHATEAU de la HAIE when Capt. C.P.Elliott received the M.C. Lieut. G.G. Elliot and 2/Lieut. R.W Rounds also awarded the M.C. and Ptes. Jacques & Beardsell the M.M.; but were not available. Battalion moved to "Y" Huts, near ETRUN. Transport lines at ETRUN.	
	14th to 18th		Battalion moved to No.5 Camp, HENDICOURT. Prepared to move at 2 hours notice. Division	
	19th	3.30.p.m.	moved to GOMIECOURT (in tents).	in the
	21st		Battalion entrained at ACHIET le GRAND and detrained at FINS.	
	23rd		Marched to EQUANCOURT. Schemes for Officers.) Reserve Corps.	
	24th) 25th) 26th) 27th)		Training carried out at EQUANCOURT. "D" Coy: attached to 470 Field Coy: R.E. at GOUZEAUCOURT for Camp Building. "A", "B" & "C" Coys: moved to VILLERS PLOUICH to work under 232nd Army Troops Coy: R.E. but were ordered to return to EQUANCOURT. "D" Coy: return to EQUANCOURT.	
	28th		Battalion standing by.	
	29th		Battalion moved to old British Front Line in front of BEAUCAMP. In bivouacs.	
	30th		Battalion moved to GOUZEAUCOURT and advancing to BEAUCAMP. Battalion took up position in Heard Bosche was in GOUZEAUCOURT and advancing to BEAUCAMP. Orders received from Brigade to move into Unseen Support Line. old British Front Line.	

[signature] Lieut:
for Officer Commanding,
2/8th Battn. THE SHERWOOD FORESTERS.

APPENDIX.

EXTRACT FROM 59th Divisional Intelligence Summary, 2.11.1917.

"OPERATIONS.
"   Further details of the enemy raid on No.5.Post at N.27.c.2.0.
"have now been received.
"   This post was an advanced post sent out at night in front of
"AVION Church, and consisted of 1 Corporal and 5 men - 6 in all.
"   At about 5.45 p.m. to 5.50 p.m. the enemy put down a barrage,
"principally of Trench Mortars.   Immediately afterwards No.5 Post
"was bombed with hand-grenades.   The trench mortars gave out a
"great deal of smoke, but according to the occupants of No.4.and 6
"posts, which were to either flank, two parties of Germans, about
"20 in each, were seen advancing and were engaged.
"   A.L.G., post to the left rear of No.6.Post also opened fire,
"and a dead german belonging to the 17th Division was picked up
"opposite this post.
"   No.5.Post seems to have received a direct hit from a trench
"mortar, and of its occupants 2 were wounded and three killed.
"These bodies have been recovered.   There remains one missing man.
"Search has been made for him without success.   It is just possible
"that he may have been taken prisoner, but as neither of the two
"wounded men saw any Germans in the actual post, he is more likely
"to have been buried in the debris".

Army Form C. 2118.

WAR DIARY
or
INTELLIGENCE SUMMARY
(Erase heading not required.)

Summary of Events and Information

2/8th Battn. THE SHERWOOD FORESTERS.

DECEMBER 1917

Place	Date	Hour	Summary of Events and Information	Remarks and references to Appendices
In the Field.	Decr: 1st 2nd		Battalion in MOLE TRENCH, RIBECOURT. (Divisional Reserve)	
	3rd		Battalion moved at night to HINDENBURG SUPPORT LINE near MARCOING. Attached to 18th Brigade.	
	4th		Consolidation of new Position.	
	5th		Battalion moved to Old British Line near TRESCAULT. Constructing shelters &c.	
	6th 7th 8th		Battalion remains in old British Line.	
	9th		Battalion moved at night to Front Line, FLESQUIERES.	
	10th		Heavy shelling all day on village. Enemy aeroplane brought down by our L.G. fire behind our Lines.	
	11th		Improving and wiring Front Line. Patrols at night.	
	12th		Heavy shelling all day.	
	13th		Relieved at night by 2/5th Bn. South Staffs. and proceeded to Support Position, HINDENBURG SUPPORT LINE.	
	14th		Working Parties during day constructing dug-outs, during night working on Front Line.	
	15th		Quiet during day, heavy shelling at night.	
	16th		Ditto.	
	17th		Move at night to HINDENBURG SUPPORT FRONT LINE.	
	18th		Move to Old British Front Line near HAVRINGCOURT.	
	19th		Battalion remains in Old British Front Line.	
	20th		Battalion moved to BARASTRE (Huts)	
	21st 22nd		Battalion remains at BARASTRE Ditto.	
	23rd		Battalion moved to "C" Camp, BEALENCOURT (Huts)	
	24th		Battalion remains at BEALENCOURT.	
	25th		Battalion moved by train to billets at MONTS EN-TERNOIS.	
	26th		Battalion commenced training. (Physical Drill, Platoon Drill, Musketry)	
	27th to 29th		Continuation of training including Range Practice, Bayonet Fighting and Bombing.	
	30th		Battalion proceeded to GOUY for Church Service.	
	31st		Continuation of training.	

Lieut-Colonel,
Commanding, 2/8th Bn. THE SHERWOOD FORESTERS

Army Form C. 2118.

WAR DIARY
INTELLIGENCE SUMMARY
(Erase heading not required.)

Place	Date	Hour	Summary of Events and Information	Remarks and references to Appendices
MONTS- EN- TERNOIS.	1918 Jany. 1st.		2/8th Battn. THE SHERWOOD FORESTERS. J A N U A R Y . 1 9 1 8 . Battalion out at Rest. Usual Training carried out in the mornings. Afternoons devoted to Recreational Training, including Cross-Country runs. Brigade Tactical Schemes carried out.	
	23rd		Brigade Bayonet & Physical Training Competition. Result :- "D" Coy. 2/8th S.F. 1st. 175 Points. "A" " " do. 2nd. 172 "	
			In the Individual Competition L/Cpl Wilson R. (97040) obtained first prize with 46 points.	
	28th		Final of the Brigade Fire Control Competition - representatives of this Battalion obtain 2nd prize.	
	27th		Notification is received that owing to the reorganisation of the Division, the Battalion is about to be Disbanded.	

	29th		Draft of 2 Officers and 53 Other Ranks transferred to the 12th Bn. Sherwood Foresters.
			      " " 19 " " 198 " " " " 2/6th Bn. Sherwood Foresters.
			      " " " " 198 " " " " 2/5th Bn. Sherwood Foresters.	

	30th		" " 2 " " 135 " " " " 1st Bn. Sherwood Foresters. " " 7 " " 85 " " " " 1/8th Bn. Sherwood Foresters.	

1.2.18.

Lieut-Colonel.
Commanding. 2/8th Bn. Sherwood Foresters.

www.ingramcontent.com/pod-product-compliance
Lightning Source LLC
Chambersburg PA
CBHW081502160426
43193CB00014B/2561